# A Spark in the Dark

by Thomas Sato
illustrated by Benton Mahan

Core Decodable 48

McGraw Hill Education

Bothell, WA • Chicago, IL • Columbus, OH • New York, NY

**MHEonline.com**



Send all inquiries to:
McGraw-Hill Education
8787 Orion Place
Columbus, OH 43240

ISBN: 978-0-02-133479-7
MHID: 0-02-133479-X

Printed in the United States of America.

9 10 11 12 KOD 24

Mom sits on the porch.
The twins whiz past.

When it is dark, the stars are out.

Carmen spots a little star.
It is not far up.

"What a star!" said Carmen.
"I wish I had that star."

"That is a bug," said Corbin.
"I will catch more in a jar."

"A spark in the dark," said Carmen.